sales MANUAL

The Successful Business Mantra of the Professionals

PAM AHUJA

An imprint of
B. Jain Publishers (P) Ltd.
An ISO 9001 : 2000 Certified Company
USA — Europe — India

SALES MANUAL

First Edition: 2010
3rd Impression: 2013

All rights reserved. No part of this book may be reproduced, stored in a retrieval system or transmitted, in any form or by any means, mechanical, photocopying, recording or otherwise, without any prior written permission of the publisher.

© with the author

Published by Kuldeep Jain for

An imprint of
B. JAIN PUBLISHERS (P) LTD.
An ISO 9001 : 2000 Certified Company
1921/10, Chuna Mandi, Paharganj, New Delhi 110 055 (INDIA)
Tel.: +91-11-4567 1000 • *Fax:* +91-11-4567 1010
Email: info@bjain.com • *Website:* **www.bjainbooks.com**

Printed in India

ISBN: 978-81-319-0662-0

We all want to succeed at

'SALES'

But some of us don't

It's not that we cannot

It's only that we do not know how

'This book is all about how to be

a great sales person'

But

Always Remember

No one gets great at selling in

'A DAY'

You only get great at selling

'DAY BY DAY'

DEDICATION

With great love and affection I dedicate this book to all the people I have been associated with in retail business.

It is my earnest belief that this book can surely pay back some of the knowledge I have gained from my associates.

I further wish that this book will assist sales people to do a better job on the sales floor and serve the **'CUSTOMER'** better.

ACKNOWLEDGEMENTS

Efforts of many people bring out an accomplishment.

I thank those people with whom I associated during the last twenty years in retail management. I also thank my family for their patience and support, while I worked long hours continuously in the retail business. Also, their support was instrumental in writing this book. Many examples and motivational anecdotes are from different sources and the result of thorough research along with my personal experiences over the last twenty years.

My gratitude to B. Jain Publishers for accepting the manuscript for publication, and for valuable and timely advice on improvement in several aspects.

Take Criticism Positively

And

Do Higher Quality Work

IN THE 'WORLD OF BUSINESS'
A SALESPERSON IS THE
'MOST IMPORTANT PERSON'

TEN COMMANDMENTS OF SELLING

1. Smile at customers.

2. Speak to customers.

3. Be Friendly towards customers.

4. Call customers by name, if you know him/her.

5. Have a genuine interest in every customer.

6. Always be cordial to customers.

7. Be generous with praise on customer's choices and selections.

8. Be considerate of customer's feelings.

9. Be thoughtful towards customer's opinion.

10. Be alert to give service to customer.

INTRODUCTION

'You cannot always buy right.
But you can always sell right'.

The retail industry in India is growing fast since the last few years and its substantial growth is manifold. It is evident in different sectors.

India is becoming economically stronger very rapidly.

India is emerging as a stronger economy and affluence is very apparent nationally as well as internationally. Its affluent middle class has lot more money at their disposal to spend.

All this makes them very attractive consumers.

Today, people dress up attractively and have better standard of living at home as well.

They are shopping for better clothes to wear.

They are also buying better quality domestic appliances.

That said, our retail industry is on the rise in a very BIG way.

To keep up with the magnitude of demand, vast shopping malls have come up in many cities and are being built in every big city of our nation.

Everything is available whether its imported or manufactured domestically.

With emerging *'Shopping Mall Culture'* we have to find ways:

- To cope with the emerging trends
- To train our sales people to take charge of the business
- To give outstanding customer-service to customers so that they keep coming back.
- To enhance business financially.

This is what this manual is all about.

In this Manual
we will elaborate on how to become:
'Professional and Successful Sales Person'.

::--------::

PUBLISHER'S NOTE

As more and more shopping malls crop up, there is clearly a 'retailing revolution.' The revolution requires selling skills, commitment to customer service, and a dynamic personality, on the part of those who seek employement in malls and department stores. This book aims to instruct new employees of stores in the art of salesmanship and customer service. There is cut throat competition among stores and malls, each trying to outdo the other in product pricing, superior customer service and business and market intelligence. Unquestionably the stores want the most pleasing personalities and best sales & marketing talent. The author herself has decades of retailing experience in USA, which has made her an authority on retailing. Even as the author uses time-honoured and inspiring quotations to motivate the readers, she addresses the prime question of the type of personality most required by stores- an organized and disciplined person, well dressed with a positive attitude, high aspiration and achievement orientation and so on. But since retailing required excellent

PR skills, a capacity for self control and restraint would indeed translate into money for the store in the long run.

This book, then, provides yeoman service to the new profession of retailing, and instructs both employer and employee in what makes a department store a winner in all areas of the game, and what keeps it at the top. The high professional standards, the sense of direction and a global vision that the author champions will become the main stay and emblem of any economy, and save it from stagnation and a lack of vision.

Kuldeep Jain
CEO, B. Jain Publishers (P.) Ltd.

CONTENTS

Dedication iv

Acknowledgements v

Introduction ix

Publisher's Note xi

CHAPTER-1
Pure Selling Environments 2

CHAPTER-2
Professional Occupations 28

CHAPTER-3
Be Customer Ready 34

CHAPTER-4
Opening the Sale 40

CHAPTER-5
Overcome Objections 46

CHAPTER-6
Closing the Sale 52

CHAPTER-7
Art of Handling Returns 58

CHAPTER-8
Art of Customer Development 64

CHAPTER-9
Store Security Issues 70

CHAPTER-10
Selling with Positive Attitude 76

CHAPTER-11
Sales and Sales Signs 80

CHAPTER-12
Retail Revolution 88

CHAPTER-13
Telephone Etiquette at Workplace 94

CHAPTER-14
Body Language and Tone of Voice 102

CHAPTER-15
How to Reduce Stress at Workplace? 108

CHAPTER-16
Facts of Retail Employment 114

CHAPTER-17
Personal Skills (Employer Seeks) 121

CHAPTER-18
Proper Training Creates Winners 127

CHAPTER-19
Author's Final Thoughts 134

Be Professional
Dress Professionally
Look Professional

CHAPTER -1

PURE SELLING ENVIRONMENT (PSE)

'Think right toward customer'.

PSE is a move to focus entirely on sales and customer service. It is a team driven system that requires the co-operation and participation of every member of the team.

Today, the competition is great. Every store is fiercely working to outdo the store next to them. The customer has greater variety of choices to shop. The mall has lot of shops with similar merchandise. One shop might sell a top with a little sequin on it, other might have little embroidery on it and another might sell just a well tailored shirt. The big question is : why should a customer buy from you? It all boils down to you as a salesperson. To be a successful salesperson depends entirely on your ability to open up the customer, to communicate and satisfy the customer.

To be a successful retailer pure selling environments (PSE) have to be created. PSE has three main aspects for success:-

1. Professional selling skills
2. Customer service
3. Teamwork

> 'All these aspects go hand in hand and neither can stand alone and win'.

1. Professional Selling Skill

One key ingredient of pure selling environments is selling skills. Polished selling skills give you an edge over the competition.

In today's retail environments a salesperson is not a clerk anymore, he is a professional who needs to develop special selling skills and go the extra mile to cultivate the customers. Your goal as a professional sales person is to create a desire in your customer to want what you have to sell. The main ingredient for a successful salesperson is preparation, preparation, preparation.

Preparing yourself as a professional is to know your merchandise, price structure and your competition. What your competition is selling, their good points and bad points versus your merchandise. Be ready to talk about your competition and be confident about the product you are selling.

Types of Selling skills :

(a) **Approaching the Customer** – Approaching the customer is how you make initial contact. Basic and professional levels of approaching the customer are as follows:

BASIC	PROFESSIONAL
• Approaching customers promptly.	• Finding the customer first. Seeking out, approaching and greeting customer as they enter your department.
• Showing customers you are happy to see them.	• Smiling, standing with confidence and maintaining eye contact.
• Greeting customers with a personal welcome.	• Greeting customers with a warm and personal welcome.
	• Introduce yourself.

(b) **Identify needs** – Basic and professional levels of identifying the customer's needs are as follows:

BASIC	PROFESSIONAL
• Asking the customer direct questions that are related to the merchandise to discover their shopping needs.	• Noticing what customers are interested inor looking at.
	• Using personal stories to encourage customers to reveal their shopping needs.
• Listening to the customer. questions as	• Asking open-ended or direct appropriate.
	• Listening attentively and maintaining comfortable eye contact.

(c) **Showing the merchandise** – The key to showing the merchandise is knowing the merchandise. In order to show the merchandise you need to be able to translate features into benefits. Think of a feature as what the product HAS; a benefit as what the product DOES.

Pure Selling Environment

BASIC	PROFESSIONAL
• Walking your customers to the desired merchandise. • Assisting with the selection process. • Directing customers to another area of the store if merchandise is not available in the department. • Discussing basic features and benefits of each product shown.	• Showing specific merchandise to satisfy customer's needs. • Pointing out features and benefits that are important to customer. • Observing the customer's interest level and responding with additional information or suggestions. • Matching the customer's needs with right merchandise. • Selling what the customer needs. • Suggesting related merchandise or complementary items such as merchandise necessary to complete a project and maintenance agreement etc. • Describing the price and value of purchase.

(d) **Completing the sale** – To complete the sale you need to recognize when customers are ready to buy and then ask for the sale. Basic and professional levels of completing the sale are as follows:

BASIC	PROFESSIONAL
• Asking for your customer's commitment to purchase. • Completing the transaction quickly and efficiently at the register. • Thanking your customers by using their names when they charge or pay cash or cheque.	• Asking for your customer's commitment to purchase. • Overcoming any customer objections by suggesting new approaches, ideas or solutions. • Acknowledge waiting customers.

Satisfied Customer is Customer for life

CUSTOMER SERVICE

NORMAL STANDARDS	PROFESSIONAL STANDARDS
• Telephone calls should be answered.	• All calls should be answered within three rings.
• Customer calls should be returned.	• All customer calls should be returned within 24 hours.
• Pay undivided attention to your customer.	• You should make eye contact with your customer as soon as he/she enters your department.
• When a customer is upset be polite.	• You should always apologize and show empathy when your customer is upset.
• Personalize your service by being polite.	• Personalize your service by giving your name and using customer's name to thank at the close of the sale.
• Always dress nice.	• Being professionally dressed gives your customers a nice feeling to deal with you.

THE MANTRA FOR
GREAT CUSTOMER SERVICE

- The Customer is Job Number One.

- The Customer is King.

- The Customer is Always Right.

2. Customer Service

It is a well known fact that companies or stores who give good customer service stay in business and flourish. There is no substitute for outstanding customer service. Always put yourself in customer's place and take care of them. Treat them as honoured guests in your home.

(a) **Satisfy every customer** – Greet every customer with a smile. Make every customer feel comfortable and give impression that you are happy to see them in your store. Make them believe that your sole purpose is to assist and satisfy his or her needs for that day. Make eye contact as it shows that you know your job and are confident about assisting them.

There is always a customer who got away, whom you were not able to sell anything. But there will always be another customer whom you will be able to sell, which will make your time worthwhile. The most important thing is to learn from your mistakes. Mistakes are good mistakes if you learn from them and improve upon your customer service.

'Always remember that in retail there are no big mistakes which cannot be rectified'.

Every customer should be welcomed as it is a part of your job. They should not be considered as an interruption to your job as they are your job. Never forget they are the only reason you are there. Always remember they pay your salary.

Your company spends hundreds and thousands of rupees on merchandise, location and advertisement. For them it flatly makes sense to sell to every customer who comes through those doors. Sales-person's pride should be to try to convert every shopper who walks through those doors into a customer.

So go ahead and 'wow' every customer and go that extra mile to satisfy every customer. How good a sales-person are you? Answer lies in how many times you went to the cash register to ring and close the sale.

(b) **Personal problems off the floor** – Do not bring your personal problems from home or from outside the doors of your work place. Your customers are not bothered about what happened to you at home or on the way to work. So always smile and greet your customers courteously and pleasantly.

As a customer when I go to a shop I expect prompt and courteous service, in the same fashion I should provide prompt and courteous service to all my customers in my store.

Believe me that every customer has HIS or HER problems. May be that is what she is trying to escape and came in to shop to uplift herself or have to change her mood. So as a sales-person you should give your very best which she is entitled to and deserves.

It is the bench mark of professionalism if you can perform regardless of your problems and at the same time satisfy your customer.

'When you are worried you accomplish less'.

(c) **Do not socialize on the selling floor** – It is easy to get-together when you see your fellow associates and discuss last night's game, T.V. show or any personal conversation when it is slow on the sales floor but always remember that you are not paid for that. You are there to take care of your customer.

'Selling floor is not Meeting floor'.

It is true that you cannot control the moment when customer comes into your store but you certainly cannot bring them back, if they leave feeling unhappy and upset. You can always have conversation with your associates later. Selling floor is never an appropriate place to congregate, specially when there are customers in the store. A customer should never feel that your conversation with associates is more important than their business.

'Customer always comes first'.

So make it a rule for everyday that there is nothing more important than customers, when you are on the sales floor. There should be an 'unspoken law' to stop all conversation when customer walks in regardless of how important it is, so you can pay undivided attention to the customer and SELL, SELL, SELL.

(d) **Acknowledge every customer's presence** – It is very important that every customer who walks into your store or department be greeted at least with a simple 'hello', even when you are helping another customer. It makes the customer who is waiting feel welcome and know someone will assist them when needed.

ALWAYS SHOW THE CUSTOMER THAT 'HE IS IMPORTANT'

Customers do not like to disturb the salesperson who is busy. If not acknowledged and assisted in time he or she might wait for a while and leave, never to come back.

Just like in the party at your home, you would like to greet every guest who walks in, even though you are engaged in conversation with another guest, with a wave of hand, smile or a nod. Similarly acknowledge every customer's presence at your store.

Acknowledging the customer has its beneficial side effects, as it will deter theft in the retail store. If a customer is acknowledged upon arrival, they are less likely to attempt shop lifting.

> **'Shop lifting depletes inventory and reduces the profit margin'.**

(e) **Never qualify a customer** – The number one rule of retail is never to judge the customer as he enters your store. Do not make up your mind whether this customer is going to buy or just browse, because of the way he or she is dressed or speaks.

> **'Customer can surprise you'.**

Being in this profession, I have witnessed this on several occasions. One time around 'Valentine's Day' one customer dressed very casually came into the store and my fellow associate did not pay much attention. When I observed that I took over and greeted the customer pleasantly and started talking to him. After asking a few probing questions I ended up selling him six outfits and matching jewelry, so never judge before you make contact with the customer.

There are top ten list of prejudices, most sales persons fall for :-

1. Quality of clothing
2. Age
3. Gender
4. Language
5. Accent : Local or foreign
6. Race or religion
7. Mannerism
8. Facial features
9. Weight
10. Hair style and over-all looks

In my opinion there is an 11th one, which is the most important one – That a customer who comes in almost every day and buys very seldom. We tend to ignore him/her and he/she might surprise you one day and become your 'customer for life'. So never judge any customer who walks in the store. A professional salesperson should always greet every customer pleasantly and try to find out the needs of the customer and fulfill them.

(f) **Give customer his/her personal space** – You will find some customers very friendly who will respond to your greetings with enthusiasm whereas other customers may feel uncomfortable when you get too close to them physically or verbally. So you should approach every customer very carefully. Definition of personal space is different with everyone. Physically-for some customers two feet is comfortable whereas for others your being on the same floor is too close. It all depends on what kind of day the customer has been having. Remember, his/her mood swings may have nothing to do with you personally. So do not take this personally and approach very carefully.

'Customers are adverse to pushy Sales Persons'.

Verbally greet your customers pleasantly to avoid violating his/her private space. Exchanging names in the beginning may label you as a pushy sales-person so you should wait till the customer finds something he/she is interested in. Customers generally do not appreciate pushy sales people, they might get put off and leave without buying. During demonstration you can exchange names and ask probing questions to find out their needs. There is a simple test of finding your customer's name and how formal or informal he/she is.

Introduce yourself first by saying : My name is Pam and wait for the response. Generally there are three possible responses – First, if the customer responds : I am Nikita. That means she is comfortable with you addressing her by her first name.

Secondly, if the customer responds : I am Mrs. Gill. That simply means you have to be a little more formal. Finally, if the customer response is : That is nice. That definitely means he/she is extra formal and you should be very careful and respect his/her personal space. At this juncture you should simply say : I will be around if you need any assistance, please let me know and walk away. Get busy doing something on the floor where he/she can see you. Do check back with him/her if

Even though

'LISTENING'

is the hard part

'YET'

Listening is the most

important part of Selling

**'KEEP LISTENING
TO LEARN'**

they are still looking. This gesture will make her feel warm towards you and think that you care and are sincere about your profession. You can learn a great deal about a customer from their body language and the way they respond to your comments and gestures. In retail numerous sales have been lost due to sales people violating customer's personal space unknowingly. Avoid being too formal. Because being polite and courteous will bring you more sales.

(g) **Listen more, talk less** – Most customers know what they are looking for. They may not know the correct or technical names of the items they are looking for. A sales person should know and take pride in knowing the technical names for the product, this is where a sales person has to be very careful, not to correct your customer right away. Listen carefully and pay your undivided attention to the customer and identify the needs of that customer. For example a house wife may not know the difference between a VHS and a VCR. Correcting her right away might make her feel incompetent and she may not buy anything. Yes, it is important to let her know the difference. Explain to her, while talking about the features and benefits of the product in the process of closing the sale. So timing is very important.

'More you listen,
more information you gather'.

Always use the language he/she understands. Avoid using big technical words to prevent misunderstanding and confusion. If you have to use them, then always explain in simple layman's language. For example the associate selling diamonds in jewelry department uses words like 'inclusion' (natural black spots in diamonds). Most of the times customers are not familiar with technical terms and they will hesitate to clarify as it will show their ignorance. So instead of clarifying they will leave with the promise to be back. But we all know he/she will not come back.

There is always an exception to this rule – If the customer is well informed, sales person will have to use trade terms to speak at their level to gain their respect and confidence so they feel comfortable buying from you. Always compliment them on their knowledge and purchase.

Also it is important, never to interrupt, correct or make a point when customer is speaking. This can have a very negative effect and may result in sale loss. Always remember to listen and wait for your turn to speak.

(h) **Always dress up professionally** – First impression is always the best. As soon as the customer enters in the store (always remember, he/she came in to buy) even before your greetings, they form their opinion about the store, all merchandise and you as a sales person in the store. So it is specially important that every item should be displayed properly, neat and clean and you look your best and cheerful. Certain things are beyond your control like customer's frame of mind, personal problems or pre-conceived ideas about the store.

Obviously, a store that looks like it needs tidying up and dusting is not as inviting to shop as a store

You are not fully dressed

until you wear

'A SMILE'

which is well organized, neat and clean and well lighted. Similarly sales people need to be well groomed, dress professionally and support a friendly welcoming smile. So the clean store and well groomed sales people show respect for the customer and are ready to sell.

'By dressing up professionally you impress the Customer'.

(i) **Always be in control** – No matter how clean the store is and well groomed sales people are, unless you have a control on your selling process nothing will work. Lack of product knowledge can result in NO SALES.

'Selling skills and People skills go hand in hand'.

Control can be maintained in any sales presentation, if the following items are in place –

1. Understanding of the selling process completely: It is very important to be a successful sales person.
2. People knowledge: to know how to approach a customer, greet them and read their body language.
3. Product knowledge: it helps you to stay in control of the sale, if you have complete knowledge of the features and benefits of the product you are selling.
4. In-Stock knowledge: you should have complete knowledge of what you have in-stock and its store location.

'Do not do guess work but have complete knowledge of availability of stock at hand'.

I remember a sales person selling a T.V. which was not in the store and was not available for next six months. Supplier had already informed the store of non-availability for that T.V. due to manufacturing problems. The customer was so upset that the store lost him for ever. It is human nature to remember a bad experience for a longer period of time and narrate it to friends. With the result that these friends of the unsatisfied customer will also hesitate to buy from this store.

'Word of Mouth gets Around Quickly'.

So it is very important that every customer leaves the store happily and is fully satisfied with the purchase.

'Create a great experience and make a customer for use'.

(j) **Show confidence and enthusiam** – Even though selling merchandise you like is lot more fun than selling merchandise you do not like, but do remember that every customer has a choice of his/her own. You should not form an opinion about the merchandise. Let the customer decide.

'Customer's choice matters the most; not what you like or think is best'.

When you can sell old items or the items you do not like with the same enthusiasm as the item you love, then only, you can call yourself a professional sales person. For example if you are a jewelry sales person and you have a customer who has been saving up for a diamond ring as it is a major purchase for her and that ring is not one of your favorite items in the jewelry display case but customer is really enthusiastic about it. Then join in with her enthusiasm and show her that ring with the same energy that you would sell something you like in the case. Listen to your customer and show enthusiasm while you assist her with the items that she likes. You must explain the features and benefits and let them select the items. After their selection you must compliment them on their choice and complete the sale.

Always start your journey of selling with the certainty of the sale and sell with confidence. Do not pre-judge about the sale which can result in no sale. But if you are doing everything right with great deal of enthusiasm and still you are not able to sell, it is time to think about what you could have done differently and improve upon your presentation next time while learning from your mistakes. Remember in RETAIL there are no big mistakes which you cannot convert into positive assests in your next presentation.

So I hope that you realize that selling skills and customer service are the backbone of P.S.E.

3. TEAMWORK

The last aspect of 'Pure Selling Environment' is Teamwork.

(a) **Be pleasant** – Always create an atmosphere pleasant and conducive to shopping for your customer. Always be friendly and courteous to the customer. Make sure to welcome every customer with a smile like you would welcome a guest in your home. If a customer is happy and comfortable he/she will end up buying more than what he/she came in for.

'TEAM-WORK'

while working as a team

you must care for one another also

you got to **help** each other to achieve

'BIGGER GOALS'

always set your goals higher and

try to exceed them.

(b) **Get along with co-workers** – It is important to get along with your co-workers on the selling floor. Because if you are friendly with your co-workers, you will create a friendly environment for your customer to shop. But if there is friction between the co-workers the atmosphere will be tense and unpleasant which customer can sense easily and will feel uncomfortable to shop. It will be a loss of sale for you as well as for the store.

(c) **Do not talk bad about your co-worker to customer** – If you have a disagreement with your boss or fellow co-worker; never show to your customer or talk about it front of him/her.

(d) **Bad mood gives negative vibes to customer** – Any problems at home can put you in bad mood which customer can sense while you are selling, so leave your personal problems behind while at work.

Similarly customers come into shop for many different reasons. One of them might be to forget their problems and cheer themselves up by buying new items. So your bad mood might get her upset with you without any reason. So it is important that as a professional sales person you should keep your cool and handle the situation calmly. YOU and only YOU can change the situation into positive one with your positive attitude.

(e) **Teamwork can help you win** – Teamwork is: if you see your co-worker in a difficult situation while selling, go and assist him/her to get out of the situation.

> 'Always remember that teams can win and teamwork can help you win'.

Winning is Everything

so

Have a Winning Attitude.

Have a Clean and Well Organised Sales Floor

CHAPTER -2

PROFESSIONAL OCCUPATIONS

'Be a multi faceted sales person'.

A sales person pretending to be several different people on the sales floor can be a lot of fun. It is very interesting and fruitful. While selling to a customer I found myself to be acting like different professionals. Besides several others, there are three professions from which a sales person can benefit from while selling. These are:

(a) Consultant

(b) Builder

(c) Painter

(a) **Consultant** – One important part of being a great professional sales person is a 'consultant' who can read the customer's mind. Not in the real sense but pertaining to customer's needs for which he/she has come to the store to shop. As discussed earlier: listen more, talk less and make customer talk by saying:

'TELL ME MORE'. These three words are a great way to know the customer's needs which will help you with your presentation. As you know, a good presentation is the first step towards building a good sale.

'TELL ME MORE' also works great when dealing with 'dissatisfied customers' as this technique is very non-confrontational and makes customers open up and talk. It really helps when customer is returning or exchanging because customer is already angry when he/she comes into the store. It shows concern and gives your customer a nonthreatening opening to say what is on his/her mind. It enables you to see from customer's point of view. You should always put yourself in customer's shoes and handle it in a professional manner.

This technique will help you to find customer's needs and help him to his satisfaction, and also help you to turn an angry customer into a happy one. All this will conclude into 'Good Business'.

(b) **Builder** – A sales person is very much like a builder. Just like a builder follows the logical sequence of steps to build a building like starting from the foundation and build up. Similarly, a sales person has to have sequence of steps to follow:-

- Greet the customer
- Open the sale
- Have product knowledge
- Ask probing questions
- Do the presentation
- Overcome customer's objections

- Close the sale
- Thank the customer
- Invite the customer back

Every sales person should follow this sequence to enhance your business as well as store's. Skipping the logical sequence is like installing the ceiling before you put in the floor.

Also conversation with the customer will set the mood for your presentation and will lead to making a sale.

'Even the biggest sales start from the ground'.

(c) **Painter** – Like earlier discussed that the only thing separating your store from other stores is YOU and only YOU. It all depends on your knowledge of the product, your selling skills and customer service. You can use wonderful words to create an excitement and desire for your product in customer's eyes just like a painter who uses his brush and creates a beauty. No matter what you are selling, whether it is a brilliant diamond, camera or a style of a blouse, the words you use to explain will put buying twinkle in your customer's eyes.

You can only do this if you accurately understand your customer's needs and make them feel comfortable buying from you. You cannot sell a microwave to a customer who came to buy a camera. Likewise a customer who is interested in M.F. Hussain's painting and you try to sell him some junior artist.

To do this effectively you have to have thorough knowledge of your product so that you can paint a rosy picture of that product alongside with its features and benefits. Your skill with words will enable you to give a dynamic demonstration. With such performance you will make that customer for life for you as well as the store.

'Sense to understand what customer wants is very important'.

::--------::

Before you attain ability to see and ability to listen, you must possess

'ABILITY TO OBSERVE'

Imperative to have Product Knowledge and to answer Customer's Question intelligently

CHAPTER -3

BE CUSTOMER READY

'Preparation, Preparation, Preparation.'

To be customer ready every sales person has the obligation to walk the floor every day at the start of his/her shift. Must check the merchandise on display. To enhance your ability to be a successful professional sales person, you need to have a check sheet to follow it daily.

1. **Daily pre-check**

   It is very important to walk the floor, look for new merchandise and the price tags. Make sure that every item has a price tag, so you do not have to get embarrassed in front of the customer.

   It is also very important that you should check your back stock at the beginning of the day. You do not want to be caught into a situation where a customer asks for an item and you go to stock room only to find it is not in stock.

To avoid such situations you have to be well informed about your back stock.

Make sure your cash register has extra tape and ink pads to be ready for business that day. These are the few important issues that if you do not take care of at the beginning of the day, it might result in 'no sale'.

So working on these issues in advance may make the difference between success and failure.

2. Know prices by memory

Knowing prices by memory will help you to make a sale. While talking to the customer when the conversation is warming up and customer shows desire to buy and asks for the price if you have memorized the price or the price range of the item, quote it to the customer right away. You have a great chance of closing that sale. Stay in conversation with the customer because it will enhance your credibility, gain customer's confidence which will make you look like a professional; which customer expects you to be in the first place. If you have customer's attention you can always add on the sale. Which will be better for you as well as the store.

Let us look at the flip side of it: A nice conversation is going on and the customer wants to know the price of an item. You open the show-case and look for the price tag, but the price tag is missing and you do not know even the price range and you look lost. Meanwhile customer sees something else and loses interest in the original item. Or customer might say: he/she does not have time now and will come back. You know that they are never going to come back, hence you will lose the sale and that customer for ever.

'If only 10% of, "I will come back" customers do come back, every sales person will be rich'.

Competition is so great that customer has no difficulty spending his money elsewhere. Like we discussed earlier that difference between your store and others is: YOU and only YOU.

3. Know your competition

Today's consumers have more money at their disposal to spend but still they are looking for bargains. Today's customer shops around and knows, what is available out there and who is selling and the prices. So it is imperative that you as a sales person know your competition, their range of product, their prices, their return policies, their extra service offers and their sales promotion

Knowing your competition will give you an edge over other sales people.

I remember, I had a sales person who used to walk around the shopping mall during her break time and learn a lot about the competition. She used to tell the customers that our prices are the lowest for the same merchandise than other stores in the mall. She used to suggest and encourage them to go and check it. Sure enough most of the customers would come back and shop in our store. She had customers come in just to get her services and she was always very pleasant and the customers enjoyed talking to her because in the process she did carve a special relationship with these customers. By doing this she enhanced her sales considerably.

So knowing your competition gives you a confidence and credibility to be the expert, customers expect you to be.

'Customer Service is perception of Customer'.

4. **Product knowledge**

   As a professional sales person you have to make a commitment to know everything about the product you are selling and know the selling techniques as well.

   It is imperative to have product knowledge to answer your customer's question informatively.

   'A good sales person has done his home work before he starts the day'.

   You should know :-

   (i) Special features and benefits of the item you are selling.

   (ii) The price structure of the product in comparison to another similar item by different company.

   (iii) The warranties offered by manufacturer and by your store.

   (iv) Special care that the product needs.

   Learning all this does not take much time but it gives you the confidence in selling. A customer feels comfortable buying from a sales person who is knowledgeable and able to answer their questions like an expert. It will help you to handle customer's objections efficiently. Your knowledge will show the customer that you take pride in your job and customer will come back for more. It is a WIN-WIN situation for both, you and the store.

   So now you realize that the key to your success is organization and preparation. There is no substitute to preparation. To make sure that you and your store is ready for the customer on that day, you need to walk the floor to check house-keeping, advertised merchandise and signage to help the customer effectively. To make sure the floor is clean, well organized, customer ready and friendly. Your success depends entirely upon your communication skills, your product knowledge and your enthusiasm to sell.

'Customers are generally sales person resistant not sales resistant'.

::--------::

Opening the sale is
Science as well as Art

CHAPTER -4

OPENING THE SALE

'Opening line should be captivating to start the conversation'.

1. **Your opening line is critical**

    In my opinion, your opening statement will set the tone for your sale. Lot has been talked about closing the sale, but not much about opening statement, which is very important Opening the sale is a science as well as an art. Science is our experiences about opening the sale whereas art is to use these experiences which befits your own personality. You cannot go against your own personality, because you will not be comfortable delivering it. So every sales person has to come up with his/her own opening line to suit the personality.

2. **Customer's re-action**

    When a customer has a bad experience in a store, they label that store and everything else associated with it as bad.

They may react adversely without even realizing it. Here are some examples to explain:

Any bad or adverse experience while growing up, leaves a long lasting effect on one's personality. For example if a child falls from a horse at the age of four, he/she may not ride a horse throughout his/her life. Secondly, a sales person not having enough 'product knowledge' about the department {he/she working in} and pushes the customer to buy something which he/she is not very excited about it. Now this customer labels the sales person as very PUSHY and AGGRESSIVE. There are all kind of stories to support this.

Customers do not like sales people generally from their own experiences. I used to feel upset when any customer resented me without even knowing me. Every time I had to remind myself that they are not upset with me as a person but due to their bad experiences, while shopping they are indifferent.

Here are some of the reasons why they are indifferent:

(i) While shopping they could not find a sales person in the department, when they needed assistance.

(ii) Customer was sold on something which he/she was not looking for.

(iii) The sales person was very pushy and aggressive and literally pushed the customer to make a sale.

(iv) Sales person lacked product knowledge to overcome customer's objections.

'All these reasons are still prevalent in retail business today'.

This makes every sales person's job all the more difficult to start a dialogue with the customer. As a sales person you have to overcome their resistance and develop person to person dialogue. Once you develop person to person relationship, that customer becomes your customer for life. The customer will come back time and again, because of your personal relationship and outstanding customer service you give.

That is why opening of the sale is very important and fruitful. Always take few extra moments to start the sale. OPENING LINE should always be friendly and pleasant. Your opening line should never be where customer can answer with simple YES or NO. Best opening line is which is not business related. Talk about the weather, beautiful morning, nice and bright day or talk about the mall; if it is busy or slow. If a customer has a child with him/her, compliment on the child, which is the best way to start the conversation. Once the conversation gets going you can gear it towards the purpose of visit to store.

For example, you can say, are you looking for something special? Can I assist you to look for it?

But once again, you are on the front line with the customer. You are the best judge on how to approach that customer and make small talk, which will relax both you and the customer with each other. Develop your own approach that you are comfortable with. But one thing is for sure, that your opening line or approach will set the tone of the sale.

'Opening line should be pleasant and sincere'.

Practise few opening lines over and over, till you find few you are comfortable with. Opening line should be unique, sincere or different enough to cause a conversation. Shopping for some customers is either an entertainment or a big hassle. Generally, people like shopping malls and it will be great if you take time to make it fun for them and yourself. Create an environment, where you and the customer have fun and also customer spends lot of money to buy more than he/she came for.

::--------::

Most people buy for their own reasons, not your's so it is upto you to find out **THEIR'S FIRST**.

Product knowledge is the key to your success.

With Product Knowledge you can ask probing question to help.

CHAPTER -5

OVERCOME OBJECTIONS

'Give every customer your ears,
but to few your voice'.

Today, in retail business no sale is complete without customer's objections, but objections do not mean that the sale is lost. As a professional sales person you have to handle these objections tactfully to complete the sale. To overcome the customer's objections you have to understand their needs for that day and what they are looking for.

1. Ask probing questions

It takes a professional sales person to find out what the customer wants and his motivation for wanting it. Once you are comfortable with your opening lines and are confident to use them with your customer, it still does not guarantee you the final sale. Opening conversation may help you to find out what the customer is looking for and still you have to find it why and who is it for. This will help you to make your presentation very effective. As a skillful sales person you will have to determine the reasons for the potential sale and ask probing questions, 'as no two customers are alike and also their needs are different.'

It is of utmost importance to find out what that particular customer is looking for.

For example: two customers walk into your department to buy a suit for themselves. Customer A may he looking for a suit for formal occasion whereas customer B might be wanting just a casual suit for day to day use. Even though both customers are looking for suits, clearly their needs are quite different. If you make the same presentation to both the customers without probing, it will result in losing one or both the sales. This will cost you your commission and revenue to the company.

A professional sales person will probe first to find out the personal reasons for which the customer is buying a suit. Presentation according to their needs will help you to gain their trust . Customer will feel important and believe that you are giving them personal attention and it will help you make the sale.

2. Understanding customer's needs

A proper knowledge of their needs will help you suggest right merchandise and customer will be able to select the appropriate items for themselves. You will then be in a position to suggest the accessories to go with those items and increase the amount of sale. Remember you can always sell right.

'Always be polite while probing the Customer'.

So, the only purpose of probing is not what customer is looking for, but to establish a long term relationship between customer and you as a sales person, and understand customers needs and desires. To develop the probing skills you have to ask open ended and fact finding questions. Never ask a question where customer can answer in just Yes or No.

Always use words like: who, what, where, why, how and tell me? If you start a sentence with tell me more you will get a complete answer with lots of useful information. Close ended questions like: are you, could you and did you? Here customer can answer only Yes or No. With the close ended questions you will get the information what they want to give. So choose the right words and probe to find out their needs to help you do the presentation for the right product. It will save time for you and the customer.

3. Earn customer's trust

Always use the caring tone for your questions and empathy to their answers. Once your customer feels that you are genuinely interested in them, they will trust you and value your opinion.

Once the trust is established between you and the customer, that customer becomes your customer for life. In my opinion, probing is one of the dynamic process in selling. With this process you can get lot of extra information from the customer which you can use to do the presentation right, gain trust and close the sale. It takes a skilled and professional sales person to overcome objections which customer might have, with the help of your 'product knowledge'. Once you learn the art of probing you will find out that the customer has several requirements. You can do your presentation tailoring the merchandise, its features and benefits to your customer's needs. Your presentation should bring excitement in your customer's mind.

Your 'product knowledge' and sticking to the customer's needs will earn his/her respect. They will be more attentive and they will pay more attention to your presentation.

You should use very sincere and polite tone of voice which will help you earn customer's trust and respect. Earning customer's trust and respect is very important part of selling and making a customer for life.

EVERYONE IS A WINNER

The customer wins by:
1. Enhancing his/her wardrobe.
2. Feeling good about the purchases.
3. Enjoying the shopping experience.
4. Gaining confidence in the product and the service.

The sales person wins by:
1. Receiving higher sales/higher commission.
2. Gaining confidence in a job well done.
3. Feeling good about the company.

The company wins by:
1. Higher sales/higher profits.
2. Gaining positive image in the market.
3. Enjoying higher name recognition.
4. Having the loyalty and respect of the associates.

Always say to the

Customer

'I AM HERE TO HELP'

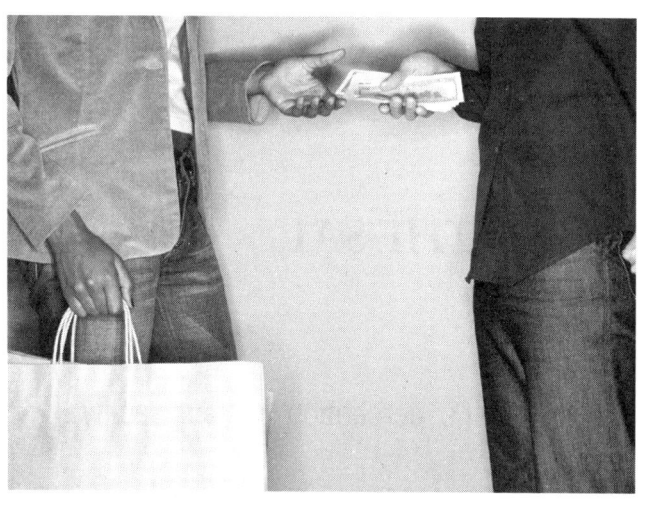

Most important part of selling is 'Closing the Sale and Satisfying the Customer'.

CHAPTER -6

CLOSING THE SALE

'Customer's perception is your reality'.

Closing of the sale is the most important part of selling. This brings revenue for the store out of which your salaries are paid and overheads are met. So if you want to get paid regularly and want your store to stay in business, you should take pride in closing every sale.

1. Sales should come naturally and easily

Like the 'opening sale,' there is no one formula for closing the sale. Every customer is different. They all have variable needs and objections. So you are the best judge on the floor while taking care of the customer to know, what is right or wrong for that particular customer. Now that you have shown professionalism and followed all the selling steps in your presentation, the sale will come naturally.

By the end of your presentation the customer should feel compelled to say, 'I will take it'. Actually closing the sale should be the least important step in the selling process.

There is always a customer who will not come out and say: 'I will take it'. That is where your salesmanship will help make the sale. Now is the time to find out the outcome of your presentation.

If you are ready and fully equipped to overcome customer's objections the first rule is to be a very attentive listener, keep eye contact, understand and acknowledge their objections. This is where your 'product knowledge' will help you complete the sale. You should know your product well, its feature, its benefits and price point. Once you have completed your presentation, ask for the sale by saying, 'shall I pack it?' And ask for the mode of payment.

'Your confidence will always bring you sales, sales and more sales'.

2. **Add on sales**

When customer shows intentions to buy, that is when you should always suggest related accessories for add on sales. Once customer trusts you, he/she will value your opinion always and buy whatever you suggest. For example:

(i) If customer has already selected a suit for himself and he is feeling quite comfortable the way you treated him so far, he is more than likely to listen to your suggestions. So go ahead and gather the related accessories for the suit i.e. shirt, tie, cufflinks, pocket square, socks, shoes and a belt. Put it on the display table so he can have a pretty good idea, how it is going to look on him. With the right selection of accessories, I am pretty sure you will enhance your sale.

(ii) Also if a lady is interested in a particular necklace, you can always suggest matching ear rings and a ring to go along. Also talk about the promotion of the week. Chances are, she will buy or come back for the complete ensemble that you have put together. Add on sales means more money for your pocket and additional revenue for the store.

3. Compliment the customer's purchase

Once a customer makes his/her choice, you should always appreciate and compliment on their purchase. Always invite them back to shop with you in the future. As a professional sales person you should have a log book, where you register all addresses and telephone numbers of your customers. It will assist you to keep in touch with your customer for future. Furthermore, to let them know of your new arrivals and upcoming promotions in the store. This will make your customers feel important and develop a data for all your customers to enhance your business.

4. Believe you can!!!

As a sales person you have to believe in yourself, 'that you can sell'. Every morning before going to work look into the mirror and feel great about yourself. Say to yourself, 'Today is the day when I am going to make that big sale, which is every sales person's dream.' Most important is that you believe:- 'You can sell and you will sell.'

This confidence comes, only if you are customer ready every day. You have the sales techniques ready for the customers and have the product knowledge of the product you are selling. As mentioned before you should have the facts ready about the features, benefits and the price point of the merchandise you have to sell. You should be ready and fully equipped to overcome the objections your customer might have. Always come across as a very sincere and helpful sales person to every customer you are selling to.

So believe in yourself and feel that you can get this sale. And you will get it. Show your confidence through your thorough professionalism.

'Everyday set your goals high and try to exceed them'.

::---------::

Do not focus on obstacles

it will result in

'Missing Opportunity'

Try to Convert Every Return into a Sale

CHAPTER -7

ART OF HANDLING RETURNS

'Listen without interruption'.

In retail business taking care of returns after sales is most tricky business. A customer who wants to return merchandise he/she bought starts building his/her case the moment he/she is ready to come to your store. By the time customer reaches your store they are already convinced that you are going to say 'No' to the return. When he/she reaches your sales counter, the customer generally is upset (as discussed in earlier chapter briefly) and at this stage you should act like a counsellor. Be very polite and patient. Listen to the customer's complaint without interruption and empathise with customer once in a while. Once you have convinced the customer that you are on their side and trying to assist, always put yourself in customer's position and see what you would like salesperson to do for you. For example, if a customer walks into your store with a 'blouse' from your inventory, which has a rip in the sleeve after first wash. You should show sympathy and exchange the 'blouse'. Thank her for her patience and apologize for inconvenience. This way you have enhanced customer's shopping experience in your store and in the process made a customer forever.

Here are some scenarios from different departments :-

(i) A customer has brought a 'blouse' to return which shrank, because the washing instructions were not followed. She probably knows that she is at fault but she starts off at you, saying, 'your merchandise is of poor quality'.

Such customers are mostly impolite and always try to put the store down.

You as a salesperson have to be very calm and calculated. Always answer 'Yes Madam' or 'Yes Sir' while listening very patiently. At this point act like a judge. Do not argue because you will not be able to prove whether or not the customer followed washing instructions as per label. So it will be better to exchange the blouse.

This will create a better relationship with the customer which will be beneficial for you and the business in the long run.

Once you win the confidence of this customer you must explain that she must follow the 'washing instructions' as per label.

'Master the Art of Returns by being Polite and Patient'.

(ii) Returns in jewelry department is very different from apparel department. A jewelry sales person should be trained to be vigilant and alert while selling and returning the jewelry. There can be lots of fraudulent returns if a sales person is not very careful while selling. A jewelry sales person should be properly trained. He/she should know how to test diamond jewelry. Diamond tester should be readily available in jewelry department. Before completing the sale diamond should be tested in front of the customer so the customer is fully satisfied.

Also the 'return process' should not start without testing the diamond in front of the customer.

Once one of my sales persons did not test the diamond in front of the customer while selling. Customer brought back a man made diamond and claimed that it was sold as such. We tried to talk to the customer that we do not sell man made diamonds in the store. Since, it was our sales person's mistake, we could not argue with the customer. In the process store had to bear the loss.

So it is extremely important for a jewelry sales person to be very careful while selling and returning.

Due to the fact that diamond buying is a major purchase for the customer, therefore a sales person should be very pleasant and cheerful. It will result into a very happy shopping experience for the customer. Sales person should be well dressed, pleasant, well trained and confident.

Confidence in a sales person is very important because a customer would like to make a major purchase of their life from an expert.

'Every return is an opportunity for a new sale'.

Art of Handling Returns

(iii) Returns in electronics and appliances are very clear and regulated. Every electronic Item has a specific 'warranty' which comes with it. Sales persons of those departments should know their merchandise and the 'warranties' which come with the items so they explain to the customer before completing the sale. Make sure it is understood by the customer.

Sales person should look and act as a complete professional handling the returns. Do take care of the customer fully if the item is still under 'warranty'.

Apologize for the inconvenience.

But, if the 'warranty' has expired, than be very polite and explain to the customer. At this stage do offer to get the item repaired at a nominal cost. If the customer agrees, send the item to 'repair centre' and keep the customer informed regarding delivery date.

'Professional sales persons try to convert every return into a sale'.

There will always be a customer with whom nothing works, then by all means take help from your superior and satisfy the customer.

After sales, the customer service is very important to bring back that customer for more business.

It is a fact that every customer who comes in the store to return is not always polite. How you handle that customer is a key to your success. If you can turn an unsatisfied customer into satisfied customer with your polite **mannerisms** and a **professionalism** it will make you a very successful sales person.

With that positive attitude you will climb the progress ladder really fast in retail business or any other business.

There will always be a customer, with whom nothing works. You have tried everything within your knowledge and still could not satisfy that particular customer. At such stage take assistance from your supervisor to resolve the issue and satisfy the customer.

'A satisfied customer is a customer for life'.

You should show similar merchandise by different manufacturers to the customer who is returning to create an interest to buy. So the customer does not leave the store without buying anything. At this time you can also suggest related accessories to enhance your sales. This will bring more revenue for you and your store.

'Work doubly hard to give better service'.

'Turn every return into a sale' should be the MOTTO of every sales person. Because it is important to master the ART of handling returns.

'Correct any thing that may have caused to lose cofidence in your store "Be a Winner"'.

::--------::

Develop Customer base with Service, Smile and Product Knowledge

CHAPTER -8

ART OF CUSTOMER DEVELOPMENT

'A satisfied customer is the best customer'.

It is important that every customer who walks through the doors of the store, goes out happy with a purchase in their hands. A company spends lots of money in getting a customer into the store. Lots of work and money is spent to establish a store.

Starting from the selection of location, merchandise, sales staff and management staff, set ups in the store in different departments take lot of planning, time and energy.

It is very important that the flow of merchandise in the store should be proper and set up should be neat and clean. Visuals in all departments should be attractive to create an exciting atmosphere to shop.

A sales person should know and understand the flow of the store.

Store layout should be easy for the customer to find out what they are looking for.

Management spends lots of revenue on advertising, radio and television and bill boards throughout the city to get the customer into the store.

When a customer walks into your department, you as a sales person should try your utmost to satisfy that customer. Be cheerful, help the customer in selecting what he/she is looking for and make the sale. If a customer is happy with shopping experience with you, this customer will be yours for life.

You have come this far and have developed a relationship. You would certainly not want to let this opportunity slip by so develop customer's loyalty.

Treat every customer like a guest in your home'.

So you should maintain customer data into your files. In your files you should record :-

- Date of visit
- Name and address
- Home and business phone
- E-mail address
- Customer's preferences
- Birthdays and special events

You would want to contact the customer for future sales and promotions. Also to notify new arrivals in the store. Always ask your customer, if it is okay to call and also ask for their convenient time to contact.

Most customers feel important when they hear from you. Whenever you call and invite customers for sales promotions or new arrivals, you must tell them your availability in the store. When your customer comes into the store, you must take some time out to assist them with what ever they are looking for. After the sale tell your customer that you have greatly enjoyed selling to them.

You should also send a 'thank you note' after every small or big sale. Also you should send major festival greetings to your customers.

Treat them like your extended family. This will help you enjoy your job and have fun.

Of course, the first step for 'customer development' is to record customer's data in your personal files. So you can wish them and invite them to visit and shop with you. This helps particularly in 'big ticket department' like major appliances and kitchen appliances. To follow through after every sale is very important: for instance some of the best and loyal customers have had problems with the merchandise in the past which they bought from your store. Your prompt and friendly service made them, 'satisfied and very loyal customer.'

An experienced salesperson does not depend on the every day traffic in the store to get sales. With their preparation, customer development techniques determines the volume of business they do.

By keeping clear and up to date records of your customer's orders along with personal data you can develop 'PERSONAL TRADE' by appointment selling.

Every management likes an employee, who takes personal interest in developing the customer relations and business. Who would not like, more business, that too on employee's own initiative? So keep it going and always be a 'winner'.

With this system of 'customer development' everyone is a winner. In the process:-

(i) Customer is happy as he/she is always treated special

(ii) Sales person is happy to enhance their earnings

(iii) Store is happy as there is more revenue for them

'Always remember people who produces good results feel good about themselves'.

::--------::

Do not be too ambitious

to handle

shoplifter yourself.

Keep an Eye on the Shoplifters and Save Revenue for the Company

CHAPTER -9

STORE SECURITY ISSUES

'Shop-lifting is a worldwide phenomenon.'

Shoplifting makes a big dent into the store revenues.

It is every employee's responsibility to always watch out for shoplifters.

As discussed earlier, every customer who walks into the store or your area must be acknowledged and greeted. This greeting itself is a great deterrent for prospective shop lifters. But if you still see shop lifting in progress, do not try to handle it yourself. Contact your security personnel or your supervisor right away. Keep an eye on the shoplifter and you can assist security personnel.

It is very important that you do not act upon it yourself, as shoplifters might be armed. Security personnel is best equipped for such incidents. It is certain that your management does not want their employee's life to be in danger. To be honest, no job pays you enough to put your life in danger.

As a new employee, during your orientation you should be walked through the security department. If not, you should ask for it so you know who should you be calling for help in time of need. It is very important to familiarize yourself with the security system in your store. It will help you to keep your mind at ease to know that somebody will be there to help you in case of emergency.

Other type of shoplifting is amongst your fellow employees. All customers are not shoplifters and similarly all employees are not honest. If you witness a fellow employee shoplifting, do not try to handle the situation yourself, instead inform your security personnel. They are trained to keep it anonymous till they catch him/her red handed. Keeping it anonymous will help you to keep your relationship with your colleagues who are involved.

Do not be afraid to report any act of shoplifting, even if you are not very sure. As the job of security personnel is not only to catch shoplifters but also to prevent it, so do not hesitate to report any suspicious character in the store. Also, do report any action which you are not comfortable with.

Do remember, not to act on it yourself. Accusing anybody without proper evidence is like putting yourself and the company in trouble.

Always stay vigilant and watchful of any suspicious action going on around you. Your watchful eyes will help the store save lots of revenue.

'Vigilant and alert employees help store, save revenue'.

- One day one of my associates, Jane saw a customer, putting a pair of ear rings into her bag. Instead of informing security personnel, she went directly to the customer was still in the jewelry department. Customer got very upset and said she had all the intentions to pay for pair of ear rings. When security was called, Jane was reprimanded in front of the customer. Jane had to apologize to the customer. Customer was right to say that she was going to pay for the purchase on the other counter because she was still in the store, whether she had the intentions to pay or not, only she knew.

But if Jane would have waited to let the customer go out of the door, it would have been an act of shoplifting. This way Jane would have been rewarded for catching the shoplifter. Security personnel are trained to handle such situations of shoplifting.

Just inform the security and keep an eye on the suspicious customers.

- In clothing department, 'fitting room' is the area where most of the shoplifting is done.

So it is very important to keep the 'fitting rooms' free of extra clothes. 'Fitting rooms' should be monitored when people are going in and coming out. All apparel employees are responsible to keep 'fitting rooms' clean at all times. Everyone can help the store to save revenue by being vigilant of the respective areas assigned to them.

- In the chapter on 'returns' we already discussed about jewelry department how vigilant an employee has to be while dealing with the customers. An expert eye of a customer with bad intentions can switch a real diamond with a fake one. It can happen to the best employee. One of my best employees named Karen was showing a 'solitaire' ring to a customer. He was looking for an

Store Security Issues

'engagement ring' and asked for the most expensive ring to look at. He thoroughly looked at it, checked the prongs and the quality of the stone. After a while he left with the promise to come back. Sure enough he came back after two days when Karen was working. He wanted to see that 'solitaire' ring one more time. Karen was well trained, not to leave an expensive item in customer's hands at any time. But this customer was so talkative and friendly that she did not even think twice, when he asked to see another ring to compare. As Karen looked down to take the other ring out he switched the original 'solitaire' ring with man made diamond ring. This ring was an exact replica of the original ring. After his first visit within two days he got exact ring made with man made diamonds in silver, instead of white gold. After switching, he told Karen I still love the original ring and I will come back with my girl friend to buy it'.

Like every day at closing when we were testing diamonds with diamond tester before putting them in the locker, we found that the exact ring that customer was looking at was fake. That is when we realized that the customer had switched the ring. Actually, he never had any intentions to buy the 'solitaire' ring. He came to rob us.

Since the store policy was to have 'security cameras' to watch jewelry department at all times, that

is how we got the physical description of the customer. Security flashed the description to all the other stores of our company and the jewelry stores in the area.

He was caught within a week, as he was trying the same 'trick' in one of our other stores. This time we were lucky enough to recover our ring but next time we may not be.

Though Karen was very upset but management was not upset with her. Because such con artists can fool anyone.

Not only Karen but everyone in the entire store learned a valuable lesson. While working on the floor all employees need to be extra careful and vigilant. So it is important to put all your efforts into the job you do and make it a success.

By now, you as an employee must have realized that everyone has a responsibility to be watchful and vigilant of 'shoplifters' at all times. Greet them and make them feel comfortable. So they know, someone is always there to help.

Tips useful against shoplifter

- Do not ever interact with 'shop lifters' yourself.
- Always, report to the 'Security Personnel' or your 'Supervisor'.
- Do not ever put your life in danger.

'Security deparment should be an integral part of the store's management'.

::--------::

Think positive about the sale and you will get the sale.

CHAPTER -10

SELLING WITH POSITIVE ATTITUDE

'Always start your day with positive attitude'.

A positive attitude is not just a way of thinking but it is a discipline and a commitment. It is a commitment to be positive, think positive and speak positive. Every morning when you wake up, you should renew your commitment of positive thinking to yourself.

Once you form a habit of thinking positive, it will make you feel good inside in all circumstances.

A person with a positive attitude will always feel good about himself. He will have a very pleasant personality and disposition. He will have a sense of humor and will have an ability to find humor in anything he does. This person always makes people laugh. Everyone feels good in his company and looks forward to meeting him and talking to him. Positive attitude along with humor is a good ingredient for 'sales success.' Finding humor in what you do, along with a positive attitude will help you enjoy your job.

A person with positive attitude will always have a set of goals and an agenda to achieve that. Every morning he sets out to achieve his own goals by following the agenda he sets for himself and works very hard to exceed them. He works harder than anybody else to succeed. Just having a positive attitude and humor does not make you a successful sales person but you have to work hard also. All these three elements put together will make it easier to achieve your goals.

'Combination of positive attitude, good sense of humor and hard work will pave the way to successful selling experience for you'.

Nobody thinks he/she has a negative attitude. You should always ask yourself a few questions to find out whether you are a positive or negative person. For example :-

(i) Do you enjoy your job or think it is a boring job?
(ii) How often do you have a bad day? Do you come out of it fast?
(iii) Do you surround yourself with positive people or negative people?
(iv) Do you look to blame someone else, when something goes wrong or yourself?
(v) Do you initiate things and work on it yourself or wait for someone to tell you?
(vi) Are you a 'leader' or a 'follower'?
(vii) Do you start your day with 'can do' or 'cannot do'?

Answer these questions honestly and find out whether you are a 'positive' or a 'negative' person.

A couple of years earlier I read an article about why sales people fail in their profession.

Some fail because they do not have **proper training** to sell.

Some fail because they are lacking **communication skills**.

Some fail because the management does not give **proper support** and **encouragement** to the employees to succeed.

But a large number fail because of a **negative attitude**.

Let us not forget that everyone can work to change their negative attitude to a positive one by:-

Listening to the motivational tapes or CDs to improve their attitude towards selling. There are also seminars they can attend to motivate themselves to think positive. Surround yourself with positive thinking people.

Learn from your co workers by observing them while they are interacting with the customer in the process of selling.

If you want to succeed in your business, not only sales but any other venture in your life, the first thing you have to do is to stop making excuses for your failures. Never focus on what you 'cannot do' but always focus on 'what you can do'.

'Can do' or 'Cannot do' depends on your ability to focus on the positive or negative. If you are focused on the negative, the results will be 'negative' but if you focus on positive anticipation and positive outcome then 'positive' results will follow.

'Combination of positive attitude, good humor and sincere action will assure you of successful career in sales'.

::---------::

Right and bold sale sign help increase the sale.

CHAPTER -11

SALES AND SALES SIGNS

'Attractive sale promotions and attractive sale signs always attract attractive business'

As a sales person you must be wondering, as to why the company wants to lose money by putting merchandise on sale. They sell for less, whereas customers do not mind paying regular price if they want to buy an item.

Let me tell you a trade secret, company recovers its cost plus overhead expenses when they sell first 25% of a style at regular price. Rest of the merchandise of this style they can afford to sell for less.

Promoting the merchandise on sale helps stores three fold:-

Firstly, sales promotions attract customers into the store. Lots of customers wait for the sale to shop because they get better value for their money.

Secondly, sales promotions generate revenue for the store. Customers tend to buy more as they are getting better prices. For example if sale promotion reads:

BUY TWO, GET ONE FREE, the customer will buy three items. These items can be for themselves or for a present. This way the company gets more revenue by selling multiple items to each customer.

Thirdly, and the most important one is that sales promotions empty the shelf space. The stores can display new and fresh merchandise on these empty shelves. Customers always love new variety of items in the store. New and fresh look brings more customers into the store. They might just look for the first time but good percentage will surely come back to shop.

'Sales Promotions bring customers into the store, they buy multiple items which will generate more revenue for the store it also helps to display new merchandise on the shelves which have been emptied because of the Sales Promotion'.

The store should bring new merchandise according to the season. New merchandise excites customers, even though they are shopping for sale items. One more reason for them to come back and spend more money. Nobody wants to come in the store and look at the old and out of style merchandise. It is specially very important in the fashion industry. Stores with new fresh look and well displayed merchandise invite customers into the store to shop.

'Today's customers are very intelligent shoppers'.

Today's customers like to shop in a clean store with well trained sales people. It is very important for every sales person to be well informed about the sale promotions and be aware of the store location of advertised sale items. It is the responsibility of every sales person of all departments to make sure that the accurate sale signs are displayed on the right merchandise. Every manager should conduct a daily staff meeting to inform and prepare the sales people for that particular day. But if it does not happen in your store, it is your duty to find out, so that you are not embarrassed in front of the customer. Most of the time the customers are well informed about the sale and the sale items. It may be his/her sole purpose to buy that advertised sale item only and leave the store. If the customer asks the sales person who is not well informed he/she has a right to get upset. It will be considered a bad 'customer service'. As discussed earlier the motto of good customer service is to satisfy every customer. It is important for every salesperson to be well informed and prepared.

It is true that most big companies have different TEAMS for putting up sales signs at the start of sale promotion and taking them down when it ends. But you, as a sales person is in the front line with the customer and work face to face with the customer. It is your duty to double check that team's work, so that you do not have to be embarrassed. Accuracy of the sale sign is very important. You do not want to have 50% off on the item or a shelf which should have only 25% off sale sign. But if it happens, what should an employee need to do+, he/she should honor the sale sign and should give merchandise on sale price to the customer and duly apologize for inconvenience. Honoring your sales commitment is a great 'customer service' towards your customer.

'A satisfied customer is always a repeat customer'.

Hopefully you understand the importance of accurate sale signs on sale merchandise. Taking down the 'sale signs' is as important as putting up the 'sale signs.'

Sales and Sales Signs

If the sale is over, all the sale signs should be taken down before the store opens its doors for business next morning. Considering the size of the store today and variety of the merchandise, it is only human to miss a sign or two.

A customer picks up an item, thinking it is on sale and comes up to the counter to pay. Sales person informs that this particular item is not on sale. He/she is going to be very upset. How would you handle the situation?

In this situation I personally believe that '4A-Rule' works great with the customers:-

(i) **Approach**
(ii) **Adjust**
(iii) **Apologize**
(iv) **Act**

(i) **Approach** – This customer is already very upset, so you have to be extra careful as to how you approach him/her. First and foremost rule is to, trust the customer. He/she is not going to lie about something which can be verified by anyone in the staff.

You must be aware that this particular item was on sale day before and in all probability the sale sign was not taken down.

(ii) **Adjust** – It is very important for you to trust your customer and make him/her comfortable. At this time adjust the price to the sale price and complete the sale. There should not be a second thought to it. All employees should be authorized to take care of such customers and satisfy them. If it is a big adjustment like in electronics or high price item, you should take approval of your supervisor.

(iii) **Apologize** - After completing the sale you should apologize to the customer for his/her inconvenience. At that time you can explain to the customer for the misunderstanding for the sign not being taken down from day before. You should invite him/her back to the store to shop. By now he/she has had an excellent shopping experience with you and will come back to shop.

(iv) **Act** - Once customer leaves your counter, you should go and take the sign down right away. So that you do not have to go through this situation with any other customer. If you forget to act upon it, you will be dealing with the same situation again and again and it will not be pleasant for either you or the customer.

Hopefully you realize that all the '4A' steps are very important for rendering good Customer Service. Good customer service will bring the customers back to the store which will amount to more business for you and the store.

A few days ago I went to a food store to buy some fruits and vegetables. I witnessed a situation which I think was very poor customer service. A gentleman had a cart full of food items and then he saw drinking water bottles on sale. He picked up six bottles and brought everything to the counter to pay. The sales person informed him that water bottles are not on sale. Customer asked her to go check the 'price tag' on

the shelf. She went and checked the price tag but still refused to adjust the price. At this stage the customer was very upset and went to the floor manager. Even the floor manager had the same attitude. At this stage the customer walked away without buying anything.

Due to this unpleasant episode the store lost business of this particular customer.

Also this dissatisfied customer will go and tell many more friends and family about the bad shopping experience at this store.

All this will result into loss of business for the store and also instead of building strong customer base store can lose customers.

It is important to give excellent customer service for the store to flourish.

'Good attitude and well trained employees are the backbone of the store'.

::--------::

THE RETAIL CULTURE

In simple terms

retail culture is us and our store.

When a customer walks through our door,
what do they
SEE, FEEL and SENSE about our store.

When they leave our store,
what do they think about the quality of

SERVICE

and competence of the staff.

How do they feel about the level of

SATISFACTION

How do they feel the way we delivered

Greet every customer with a smile.

CHAPTER -12

RETAIL REVOLUTION

'Will retail revolution ever follow retail etiquette'.

1. **Retail Culture**
    (i)   An average store in America or any Western nation will accept personal cheques for amount of purchase with proper ID.
    (ii) Shelves are properly marked for styles and brands.
    (iii) All clothes are stacked by size: small, medium, large and extra large.
    (iv) Hangers have colour coded clips.
    (v)   Brand stores always keep catalogues, so if a customer cannot find a particular size or colour the sales person will duly order from warehouse.
    (vi) Customer can buy an item in one city and if he/she has to return or exchange it, he/she can return in other city in the same store.

Caring for customer should become second nature for a salesperson.

(vii) If the customer buys a gift for someone, a gift receipt is given so it can be returned or exchanged in same store of another city. Gift receipt will not indicate price.

(viii) A return or exchange policy allows you to either return or exchange within 15 to 90 days of purchase.

(ix) In case the customer has lost the receipt, some store will still honour their policy.

(x) There are other very generous policies which some stores have adopted to facilitate the customers.

None of these policies has anything to do with America or any other nation being rich. It is simple consideration towards the customer who is the main player in this whole episode of 'selling' and 'buying'.

Caring for the 'CUSTOMER' is an integral part of retail culture in America as well as other western nations. Whereas it is yet to arrive in some developing nations of the world, where the face of retail has completely changed (specially in India and China) in the past few years. To sustain the speed of changing scene of retail we will have to adopt 'Customer Friendly' ways of doing business.

Of course we have stores and malls which look like any other store in America or other western nation but once you go in to shop, the scene abruptly changes.

'Though the face of retail has completely changed and cosmetic surgery has been done'. How about the heart transplant?

2. Retail Etiquettes

(i) Even though the shops are temperature controlled but

if the 'credit card' machine does not work, it becomes a customer problem. Of course a personal check is a NO.. NO.....

(ii) In some store the merchandise sits on floors instead of properly marked shelves.

(iii) Most of the time the marked sizes are not true to size.

(iv) Clothes on hangers is becoming more common in some shops but colour coding is not there.

(v) Even some brand stores have no readily available catalogues for the customers to consult. Orders are taken verbally and sometimes put in the computer to vanish later.

(vi) There is absolutely no facility to return or exchange the merchandise in same store in another city.

(vii) Gift receipts are not heard of in the retail business in these fast developing nations.

Some sales people laugh it off when you ask for a gift receipt.

(viii) Return policies are there in some stores but are so cumbersome that the customer gets quite upset.

(ix) If you ever lose the receipt, you can never ever return the item you bought.

(x) Caring of customer policies is not an integral part of our 'new retail' culture.

When we buy international brands in fast developing nations, we pay international prices. Anything American will cost more and in the process sales person will make more on commission. Why then are Indian customers treated differently?

Specially when they are subjected to non existing return policies.

In America (where much of India's 'retail culture' has come from) every store-from humble discount outlet to the Fifth Avenue store displays signs indicating what to find where.

'Caring for the Customer should become an integral part of sales policies'.

As you walk in the store, a store attendant may greet you and let you know that he/she is there to help you find anything particular you are looking for.

Usually, the store staff has a uniform with a name tag. It makes the staff more accountable.

If we are in the process of or have adopted western techniques to welcome the new 'Retail Culture' we must therefore adopt the very workable methods too and some techniques to treat our customers better to enhance the business and take it to a next higher level of efficiency.

'Remember if there is no Customer, there will be no sales person'.

::--------::

Always be polite and pleasant when you answer telephone at your workplace.

CHAPTER -13

TELEPHONE ETIQUETTE AT WORKPLACE

'Sales persons tone of voice on the telephone will set the tone of how friendly your store is'.

If you are not dealing with customers face-to-face, then the essence of dealing with people politely and efficiently can only mean one thin. TELEPHONE ETIQUETTE!!!! Even small things such as how long it takes for you to answer your telephone and how you communicate with your customer can be a first and lasting impression. It can set the tone of your relationship with the customer. There should be one consistent way of greeting throughtout the company, as customers really like consistency. The way company employees answer the telephone will set the tone with the customer regarding the level of service he/she can expect. This will always set the tone of what type of conversation you will have with the customer. If you answer the phone promptly and politely, the conversation will go smoothly, but if you are abrupt and don't answer the phone promptly, expect the conversation to go accordingly. Correct way of answering the telephone can give a positive first impression.

There are four basic rules for telephone etiquette:

(i) The telephone should be answered within three rings.
(ii) The caller should be greeted nicely.
(iii) Give your and company's name upon answering the telephone.
(iv) Ask the customer 'How may I help you'.

Answer the phone with three rings

Three rings is an accepted standard in the retail industry. After the third ring, the customer starts to lose patience and starts having negative thoughts about the company, for example:

- The company is out of control.
- They are under staffed.
- That they are having their issue due to mismanagement of customer service.

To avoid their negative thoughts, it is very important to pick up the telephone within three rings. Even if you do not work in that department, still answer the telephone and take a message.

Greeting the caller

A greeting should always be a starting point of the conversation and it should sound friendly and courteous. Tone of your voice should be friendly and polite, as people can tell a lot from your voice. Always begin with 'Good morning' or 'Good evening' because your customer is waiting to be greeted in a friendly manner. Do not use 'Hi' or 'Hello', which is very informal and mostly used with friends and family.

Also, very important is not to make your greeting too long. For example 'Hello, it is a great day in our store'. It is sure to annoy your customer, so keep it short and to the point.

Always smile when you answer the telephone, as the customer can tell if you are a friendly sales person.

Give your and your company's name

After greeting, you should always identify your department and give your name. It should be like, 'This is women's fashions; this is Pam (your name)'. This will give the information to the customer that he/she has reached the right department and save both of your time and frustration. This will also help you to get to the problem at hand and start to help your customer faster.

If it is a direct call from outside the store, then give your company's name, so the customer knows they reach the right store and department.

> 'In today's world telephone is they way to communitate so telephone ettiquette is very important'.

Ask the customer 'How may I help you'

Saying 'How may I help you' completes the telephone etiquette which shows that you and your company are ready to assist your customer in anything he/she needs.

Another important point is to write down the customers name in the beginning on the conversation, and use it few times during the conversation. At the end of the conversation, thank the customer by name for calling.

The correct way of answering the telephone using all four basic rules of telephone etiquette is as follows:

'Good morning, women's department
This is Pam, how may I help you'.

Even the part time employees have to be trained in telephone etiquette, as they are the front line staff and the customers' first impression of the company starts with them.

How to put a customer on hold

The etiquette for putting your customer on hold will help you avoid confusion and stress as you have ten different things going on around you. The main points are as follows:

(i) Ask the customer if they would mind holding on a minute.

(ii) You should wait for a response before putting them on hold.

(iii) Inform them of the reason they are being put on hold, like you are dealing with another customer.

(iv) Inform them how long they will be on hold. This will set the correct expectation with the customer and they will not get frustrated due to the length of the hold.

(v) Thank the customer for holding before you put them on hold and after you return.

You should always take permission before putting them on hold because sometimes it is not convenient for them to hold in the timeframe you have given them. If they can not hold, ask them for their telephone number and call them as soon as possible. This way you can take care of business in front of you and then call them back so you can give that customer your full attention.

'But NEVER, NEVER forget to call back'.

::--------::

Always use

'BRIGHT

AND

CHEERFUL WORDS'

When talking to the

Customers

TELEPHONE ETIQUETTE FOR A CURSING CALLER

Every now and then you get a customer who is upset and abusive on the telephone and says words you do not want to repeat. How to handle such customers?

- You can start politely, for example 'Sir, I want to help you but I am having difficulty understanding. Please calm down and say it again.' If he/she does not calm down, say it again one more time.

- If the customer is still abusive, try saying 'Please refrain from the language you are using. It is making it very difficult to understand you.'

- If this does not bring any results, inform the customer you are unable to help him and that you will get your supervisor to assist him/her.

- Or take their telephone number and inform them that your supervisor will contact them within 24 hours.

- Final step, you must explain to your supervisor the whole situation immediately and have them call the customer within 24 hours.

WHAT'S IN A NAME?

How you should address you customer whether in person or the telephone.

(i) Listen to your customer, they will tell you how to address them. For example :
   (a) 'This is Dr. Khan' – call him Doctor
   (b) 'This is Mrs Ahuja' – call her Ma'am
   (c) 'This is Nikita Chothani' – can call her Nikita or Ms. Chothani to be safe
   (d) 'This is Brianna' – call her Brianna

(ii) When in doubt, play it safe and address your female customers as Ms. rather than Mrs. or Miss. If she wants to be called differently, she will let you know.

(iii) Always ask permission before using the customer's first name. For example, 'May I call you Nikhil'.

Remember if the customer did not like what you called them, apologize and call them what they prefer.

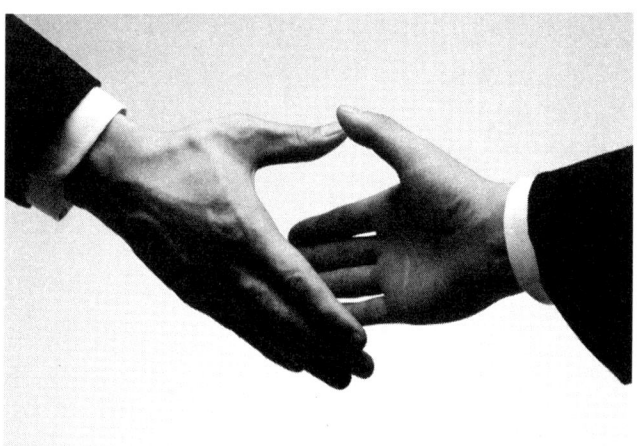

Handshake like body language tells a lot of your personality so be very pleasant.

CHAPTER -14

BODY LANGUAGE AND TONE OF VOICE

Body language

Body movements is a language all by itself and can reveal how a sales person is feeling without saying a word. Body language is a constant flow of communication without saying a word.

- Your body language tells your customer how happy or unhappy you are at your job. It will show the customer whether you are happy to serve him/her or if they are an intrusion to your work.

- Your eyes can express a lot. It is said that they are a window into what/how you are feeling. For example
    - Rolling your eyes while talking to a customer says to them that you are just listening to what they are saying because it's your job and you do not care about their problem. All you are interested in is to get back to what you were doing before.

- Making eye contact while talking to the customer on the other hand, tells them that they have your undivided attention and you are only there to help them. This will help make the customer comfortable and earn you a customer for life.

- Your face is like a mirror that reflects how you are feeling, whether you are sad, happy, excited or distracted. It is important not to bring your stress from home to work. You should always have a relaxed look on your face, which relaxes your customer also. But if you have an upset customer in front of you, you have to change your expression to concern and empathy, to show them that you empathize with them and are there to help them. So you have to adjust your facial expressions according to your customer.

- Nodding your head tells your customer you are paying attention to what they have to say without interrupting them. During the conversation, you should nod every now and then but if you nod too often, the customer might feel you want them to rush and finish their story. That might not make them very happy. Nodding up and down means 'Yes' or 'No' in different cultures. In India nodding up and down means you agree with the next person and nodding side ways means you do not.

- Hand gestures also play a big role in body language. Lot of people use their hand to express how they are feeling. Like tapping figures on something or clicking your pen repeatedly tells your customer you are bored and frustrated. On the other hand, if the customer is making these gestures, they are frustrated and want a solution to their problem as soon as possible.

So you see body language plays a big part in showing how you feel that day. You should always adjust your body language according to the situation in front of you.

> **'Every customer likes polite and courteous employee whether it is face to face or on the telephone'.**

Tone of voice

Your tone of voice takes over when you answer the telephone, face-to-face with the customer your body language conveys how you are feeling, but on the telephone, it is your tone of voice that works wonders. Through your tone of voice, it does not take very long for your customer to pick up on your attitude and mood. In fact, the customer will know about your attitude from your initial greeting, whether you are a friendly person or not, also if you will be helpful or not. Words do count but your tone of voice matters more.

- The voice that is mono toned or flat tells the customer you are bored and you have no interest in what he/she has to say.
- The voice that is slow and low pitched conveys that you are depressed and want to be alone.
- The voice that is high pitched and pleasant says I am ready to help you.
- On the other hand, if the voice is high pitched and loud, means you are angry and frustrated.

You should always answer the telephone with a friendly and smiling voice, this will make the customer feel welcomed and want to do business with you. From your tone of voice your customer will be able to tell how friendly and helpful you will be.

Body Language and Tone of Voice

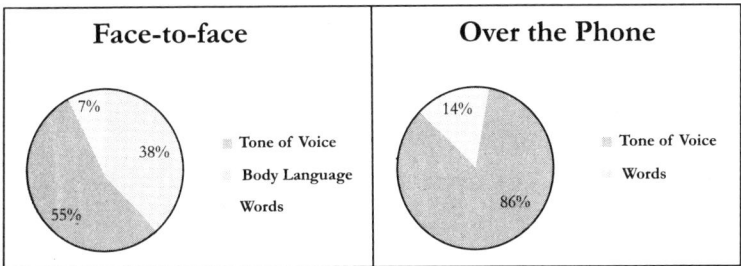

These diagrams will illustrate the importance of body language when you are face-to-face with the customer and on the telephone how the emphasis changes to the tone of your voice.

> 'Your telephone greeting should say I am ready to help'.

::--------::

Take criticism
Positively and do
Higher quality work.

Reduce stress by being positive.

CHAPTER -15

HOW TO REDUCE STRESS AT WORK PLACE?

Stress has a way to creep into any job. A sales person's job has its own stress level that can be very high at times. Here are a few ways to reduce stress at your work place:
- Change from stress talk to positive talk
- Be concerned and not worried
- Time management

'Think positive to be successful'.

Change into positive talk

It depends how you respond about a situation which will either prevent or activate your stress level.

Real life situation: As a sales person you have a customer that is demanding a refund on a dress which she bought six months ago and wore it to the party. Now she does not have any use for it and wants her money back. You as a sales person should start with a sincere apology and explain why you can not offer her a refund. The customer gets upset and asks to speak with your supervisor. Your supervisor comes and listens to the customer without interrupting. And she informs the customer that it is not our policy to accept returns or provide refunds after such a long time, but she will make an exception and bend this rule this one time, and approves the refund.

Here are the two ways you can talk to yourself, stress talk or positive talk about this situation:

Stress talk

You can put negative spin to the above situation and talk to your self by saying 'She always undermines my decision and insults me in front of the customer. She never supports me in any of my decisions. There is no use in going and talking to her.'

This talk is going to stress you further and you will end up exaggerating the situation in your mind by putting a negative label to the whole situation. You will eliminate the positives all together and stay stressed.

'Negative thoughts add to your stress level'.

Positive talk

Smart talk is a positive self talk which will create less stress and give you something positive to think about. Positive talk will go like this 'it is really upsetting but my manager has to see a bigger picture. She had to please the customer as she is a regular customer. My manager is a positive person and she is just taking care of the customer in a professional manner. It must have been difficult for her too to give refund in front of me. But I empathize with her as she did not want to lose a regular customer and by doing this, she made her a customer for life.'

While you give yourself a smart talk, you assume that your manager had good intentions, you focus on the positive and empathize with her. It will make you feel good and less stressful.

'Positive self talk helps to reduce stress level'.

Be concerned not worried

The second way of reducing your stress is to learn how to convert your worries into concerns. Lot of people waste a lot of time in worrying about the things they can not change or do anything about. These are called 'Gravity Issues'. At work place, especially large retail businesses, lot of decisions are made in the head office. At store level, you can not change those decisions whether you agree or disagree, so why worry about them and increase your stress level. It is better to leave those things alone and work around it to make your work days easier.

If you are worried about something you can not control, let it go, it will just make you feel tensed or upset. If you are worried about something you can control, then take action and turn the worry into concern. This will reduce the stress in your life and turn a negative situation into a positive.

Time management effectively

To be successful and have less stress, you have to learn how to manage your time well. Not understanding the basic principles can get you going in circles and not be able to accomplish your goals. This can be very stressful for you.

TIME
Yesterday is like cancelled cheque
Tomorrow is like promisory note
Today is like cash

Manage your time effectively to reduce stress at workplace.

Use the time management system

Start with buying an organizer, one that you can add pages to it. You can organize yourself in a monthly or daily basis like:

1. Write down all your appointments, their day, date and time. This way you will never be late for or miss your appointments. But make sure to check your organizer daily.

2. Keep a daily to do list. At the beginning of each day or the night before in case you get busy in the morning, write down all the tasks you plan to do that day, as you go through your day and complete each task then cross it out. It is also true that you will not be able to finish all the tasks for that day, so you must transfer the incomplete task to the 'To do list' for the next day. That way you will not miss any tasks. This will help you to know how much time you have for each task. This will reduce your stress and frustration for that day.

3. Prioritize your daily to do list. Your daily to do list will have certain tasks that are more important than the other. You should prioritize 'A' to the most important task (Must do) and 'B' to the less important task (Need to do) and 'C' to the tasks that are good to get done but are not important that day (Good to do). Start your day with your 'A' prioritized tasks and then 'B'. Make sure you do not spend too much time on 'C' tasks and run out of time to dedicate to 'A&B' tasks.

Three facets for to do list
'Must Do', 'Need to Do', 'Good to Do'.

Make sure you do include some personal time on your organizer. This could include time spent having fun with your friends and family, or doing your favorite hobby.

No one ever said when they get to the end of their life That 'I did not spend enough time at work.'

So be sure to make time for yourself and your family. Having long or short term plans is as important for your personal life and career.

A little long term planning saves you a lot of grief later on. As they say **'Short term pain for long term gain'**.

Get control of your time, manage it well and live a less stressful life at work and at home.

Organized people are always successful people!

::--------::

CHAPTER -16

FACTS OF RETAIL EMPLOYMENT

- Retail salespersons can expect to have better employment opportunities because of high turnover in that field every year.
- Most sales people work evening and weekends particularly during holidays.
- Employers are looking for people who enjoy working with others, enjoy work, are presentable and able to communicate clearly.

Nature of the Work

Consumers spend crores of rupees every year on merchandise. A retail sales person should try to interest the customer into buying the merchandise whether it is shoes, garments, computer equipments or automobiles. To do that, a sales person has to be prepared with product knowledge, to be able to explain features, demonstrate its use and be knowledgeable about the various models and colours.

'Product knowledge will help you to complete the sale'.

Most retail salespeople handle sales receipts, receive cash, cheques, debt and charge payments. Depending on the hours you work, you will be involved in counting the money in the cash register, separating cash from charge, and making deposits at the cash office. Sales people in such situation are held responsible and repeated shortages can result in dismissal from the company.

'For handling cash sales person should be alert and careful'.

Retailers stress the importance of providing courteous and efficient service. When a customer wants an item, do everything possible in your power to satisfy the customer. If an item is not available in your store, try to locate it in another branch or try to specially order the item for the customer.

'Every customer is a potential sale for you and your company'.

When handling returns always try to convert a return into a sale. Always be ready to suggest a substitute item in place of the return. This will boost the sales for your company.

'Try to turn every negative sale into a positive'.

To turn a negative into a positive, a sales person must exhibit a level of patience while dealing with an irate customer. Being well groomed and soft spoken will help the customer feel at ease and help you turn any situation around.

Other duties included in your job are stocking the shelves, arranging and re-arranging the sales floor, taking inventory and handling store displays.

Sales people must be knowledgeable about the current and future sale promotion to serve your customers better.

Sales people are the eyes of the company to avoid shoplifting and theft in the store and work closely with the store security department.

The retail occupation offers many opportunities for part time work for people wanting to supplement their income.

Most retail jobs require sales people to stand on their feet for long hours, especially during holidays.

Training

Most retails sales people learn their skills on the job. There is generally no requirement for having a college degree, but higher education can only help you in getting the job and doing it well. While in small stores, the training is done by the store owner him/her self. Larger businesses generally have a detailed training course. During this course, you will be trained in handling and operating the cash register, specifics of the department you will be joining, level of customer service demanded of you, store functions (store security, etc.) and interacting with customers. This training will help you be prepared to assist the customer in their shopping needs from day one.

Most stores also practise mentorship, which involves pairing a new employee with an experienced one to help them achieve a comfort level dealing with the customers. This practice will help you increase your personal confidence and better inter personal skills.

Some stores also offer periodical training for product knowledge and customer service, known as refresher courses.

> 'Improve your selling skills through refreshing your product knowledge'.

Advancement (promotions)

Opportunities for advancement vary between small stores and large companies. In a small store, advancement can be achieved rather fast due to the size of the organization, usually consisting of a few employees and the store owner, and the interaction with the store owner him/her self. Alternatively in a large company, you must demonstrate great work behavior, willingness to grow, positive ethics and results. Promotions in large companies come in the form of a position that may include salary + commission or supervisory positions.

Job Prospects

With the ever expanding mall culture in India, employment in retail businesses is readily available as retail stores are found in every city or town, regardless of size. Due to a high level of turnover in this business, there will always be a need for good experienced sales people.

During busy selling seasons like Diwali, Christmas, school breaks and other holidays, there is always an increase in opportunities for full or part time retail employment. Abundance of part time job opportunities during these times helps people who are looking to supplement their income.

> 'Part time job opportunities for people who want to have extra money'.

So the retail business is always is need for efficient and people oriented employees. **Hope it is you who gets employed next!!!**

::--------::

'ATTITUDE,' 'HUMOR' AND 'ACTION'

are three important ingredients

to

'PATHWAY OF SALES'

Always make eye contact, look and feel confident during your job interview.

CHAPTER -17

PERSONAL SKILLS (EMPLOYER SEEKS)

Every employee is looking for strong personal skills when hiring an employee for their business. Personal skills are:

Carefulness

He is looking for an employee who has abilities to think and plan carefully before starting a project. Thinking and planning reduces the chance of costly mistakes and keeps the steady work flow going. Thinking before action is a quality that helps both the employee and the employer to save time.

Cooporation

In the work place, working together and helping each other is very important for your growth and as well as the business. You should always be willing to cooperate with your superiors and other team members.

Creativity

Employers like employees who are innovative and creative. An innovative employee brings new outlook to the workplace. On the other hand, an employer should have an open mind and be a good listener, so the employees get encouraged to voice their creative ideas and put them into action.

Discipline

A sales person should be disciplined. He/she should be disciplined enough to start a project and complete it without getting distracted or bored. Never leave a project half done or incomplete. An employee should be disciplined enough to:

- start a project on time
- stay with it
- finish on time

Goal Achievers

Businesses want to have employees who have a drive to set goals and achieve them. You should have high aspiration levels and work hard to achieve them. As an employee you should always aspire to climb the ladder of management higher and higher. Through your sincerity and hard work you will be noticed by your management.

'Promotions are based on your qualifications and hard work'.

Good, Positive Attitude

A good attitude towards your work and team members results in great work performance. A pleasant attitude in the work place, results in an atmosphere where customers enjoy shopping. A customer always enjoys interacting and buying from a positive sales person. Having a positive attitude goes a

long way to productivity. Avoid negativity and negative people around you. A good positive attitude :
- Helps to complete the sale
- Develop the customer relationship
- Give great customer service

More customers results in more sales, resulting in a happy employer and more opportunities for you to succeed.

Good Will

You should have good intentions towards others and believe everyone else has good intentions. This will help you to keep your positive attitude and pleasant atmosphere throughout the work place. Spreading good will to others will result in good will towards you, helping you to enjoy interacting with your customers and team members in a friendly manner.

Leadership

Every group needs a group leader. Employers like employees with leadership qualities to guide the way so that employers can concentrate on more important things. To be a good leader you must:

- Be able to influence the group in a positive manner and be very pleasant about it.
- Be knowledgeable about the job so you can advise and guide your team members to achieve positive results.
- Knowledge of your work place and interactions among the team members is very important to help develop a positive work atmosphere.

'Be positive and create positive atmosphere at your work place'.

Organization

Well organized employee is always an asset to the company. An employee who is well organized can complete a project without distraction and road blocks. A well organized employee can complete a project without asking 'What did I do with that?' or 'Where did I put that?' If you are well organized to start with, you will:

- Save time
- Save your employer's money
- Meet all your timelines
- Complete the project ahead or on schedule

An employee should be organized and neat in what they do, big advantage of being organized and neat, you do not have to do a project twice. You can finish it in one try.

> 'Work with vigor,
> keep a rapid tempo and stay busy'.

Safe work behavior

Employers want employees that work carefully and avoid taking unnecessary risks. Create a risk free environment at work for your self and your co-workers. For example, if you are working on a project and brought some tools to complete the project. At the end of the project, put the tools back where they belong, so that no one trips and hurts themselves. These falls or hurts can cost a company big money in the way of work compensation. To avoid these unnecessary expenses companies want employees who avoid

work related accidents and not take unnecessary risks in a work environment.

Stability

One most important skill an employee should have is to

maintain composure in a stressful work situation. Customers can be upset at some other situation but make you the target of his/her release of stress. They do not know you personally, so you should not take it personally. Keep your cool and handle the situation rationally. Take your time and calm the customer down by listening without interruption. Take care of the customer and go the extra mile.

> 'Take the initiative to please the customer.
> This will help you to make customer for life'.

Appearance

Last but not least, good appearance is very important.

> 'The first impression is the last impression'.

One should always dress nice, neat and well groomed. Well groomed person gives a well organized look that every employee likes to have on their team. Customer also likes to shop with a well dressed sales person. You are judged by customers by the way you are dressed at your job. A well dressed sales person brings the following to the work place:

- Class to the work place
- Boost your confidence to deal with the customer
- Give great customer service
- Makes the customer want to purchase from you

These are the personal skills that will help you get the job and retain it for a longer period of time. These skills will help you climb the ladder of management easily and comfortably.

::---------::

Achieving good performance

is

A JOURNEY – NOT A DESTINATION

Periodical refresher course is important to give good customer service.

CHAPTER -18

PROPER TRAINING CREATES WINNERS

- Your success as a sales person depends entirely upon your ability to communicate with the customers and fully satisfy their needs.
- Establish yourself as a professional and courteous sales person, so you can build your customer base in the market.
- Create pure selling environment by developing professional selling skills, by giving an outstanding customer service and working as a team.
- By developing professional approach to selling you will be better equipped to understand customer's needs and satisfy them fully.
- Today's competition is quite fierce.
  Always be ready to talk about your competition as to what they are selling, their price structure and also their sales promotions.
- Today customers are better informed about the product. They want their money's worth for the product.

- Key to your success is 'product knowledge', know the product you are selling, its features, benefits and price structure.
- Only difference between you and your competition is the 'customer service' you extend to customers.
- Greet every customer with a smile.
- Acknowledge every customer like a special 'guest'.
- Try to turn every customer into a 'buyer' with 'customer service' and 'product knowledge'.
- Keep personal problems off the floor. They are not customer's problems but yours only.
- Do not socialize on the floor when customers are around.
- Customers can surprise you, so do not make up your mind upon their arrival in store.
- Give customers their personal space.
  Do not follow them around.
- Read customer's body language and treat them according to your judgement.
- If the customer says, 'I am just looking'.
  Walk away from him/her but do check back later.
- Talk less and listen more. Pay full attention.
- The more you listen, more information you will gather.
  This way you will get to assist your customer better.
- Never interrupt your customer while he/she is talking to you.
- Always dress up neat and clean and be professional.
- During the presentation always stay in control.
  Total understanding of selling process will help you to stay in control of sale.

- Knowledge of your product, its in-stock and its location is extremely important for you.
- Make sure the customer leaves store happy and satisfied.
- Create a 'great buying experience' for the customer and you will make that customer for life.
- Be confident and enthusiastic about the products you are selling
- Teamwork creates happy associates on the floor.
  Friendly employees create a pleasant atmosphere for the customer to shop.
- Never talk bad about your co-workers to customers.
- Always remember 'teams can win and teamwork can help you win!'
- Always assist each other on the floor.
- Salesperson's occupation is more like a consultant who can read client's mind, not in real sense but can come close to it by asking, 'tell me more'!
  These three words can get you the information you need for your presentation.
- Salesperson's occupation is also like a builder. While a builder has to follow a logical sequence to build a building similarly a salesperson has to follow a logical sequence as explained in Chapter-2.
- Salesperson's occupation is also like a painter's who can paint a beautiful picture with his paint & brush. Likewise you as a salesperson can create excitement in your customer's eyes with product knowledge.
- So, to be a successful salesperson you have to be a consultant, builder and a painter, all in a day's work.
- To be customer ready every salesperson has an obligation to walk the floor every day to look for new merchandise, displays and promotions.

- Should daily pre-check for your back stock to avoid embarrassment in front of the customer.
- Memorize the price point to improve your credibility and gain customer's confidence.
- Know your competition's product range, price point, their policies and sales promotions. This will help you to make your presentations with confidence.
- Always remember that to serve your customer with an aura of an expert, the most important steps while selling are to have 'product knowledge', 'product knowledge' & 'product knowledge'.
- As a professional sales person you have to make a commitment to learn everything about the product you are selling, its features, its advantages and also the warranties.
- Customers want to buy from a sales person who is knowledgeable and can answer valid questions.
- There is no substitute to preparation. You have to be customer ready for yourself & the store.
- Your success depends on your communication skills, your product knowledge and your enthusiasm for selling.
- Your opening lines will set the tone for your sale.
- There are no set opening lines, every salesperson has to develop their own opening lines, which they are comfortable saying.
- Practise few lines and use them to your advantage.
- Opening lines should be genuine and preferably not related to business, it should be friendly and quite pleasant.
- Customer's negative reaction should not be taken personally. It is never targeted towards you. May be this customer had a bad experience while he/she did shopping in your store last time.

- Be calm & cool while handling the customer. Give extra care.
- Customer's objections are big part of the selling process.
- Do not get disheartened because of the objections.
- Prepare yourself with the product knowledge and self confidence.
- Learn the art of probing so you can get enough information to deal with that customer with lots of confidence and intelligence.
- Always ask open-ended questions from customers to open up and give you the help you need to overcome their objections.
- Be polite and sincere to earn respect and trust.
- Once you gain customer's trust you can add on to original sale.
- Make the sale bigger by adding to it the related accessories before closing the sale.
- Add on sale means more money for you and more revenues for the store you work with.
- Always appreciate and praise the customer's choices to make them feel good for their purchase.
- Salesperson should always keep a log book to store every customer's (he/she deals with) name, address and telephone numbers. It will help you to keep in touch with the customer and also to inform them about sales promotions.
- Believe in yourself and sell with confidence.

'Believe you can win & you will win'.

::--------::

The most powerful motivation

Always comes within

'OURSELVES'

Motto of every Salesperson is Happy and Satisfied Customers

CHAPTER -19

AUTHOR'S FINAL THOUGHTS

'Customer is backbone of retail industry'.

The Mall Culture has crept into our cultural fibre in a grand way. Every big corporation has successfully gotten involved into opening Department Stores. These stores are either free standing or in the Malls. These businesses have lots at stake.

To attract Customers, the stores have to be full of inventory. Stores have to give lots of choices to the customers for them to come in repeatedly to shop.

If the inventory has no variety of merchandise, the customers do not like to shop. So you see, the store inventory should have lots of variety of merchandise.

This requires huge investments on part of corporations as well as owners.

Author's Final Thoughts

The key to set your store apart from the other stores is the customer service your employees give to the shoppers.

'A store with well trained, customer oriented, knowledgeable and well mannered employees will survive over the other stores in today's retail industry'.

Always remember repeat business is the only way to survive in today's retail industry. So it is your prime duty to give great Customer Service always, so the shoppers do come back to shop with you with enthusiasm. Customer is the only reason that you as a sales person is there. Remember they are the main source of income for employees, as well As the employer.

Things to Remember

- You should know your merchandise well. Learn the features and benefits of the items you are selling.
- You should listen more, talk less. Understand the customer's needs fully. Sell the items according to customer's need, so that there are few or no returns.
- You should trust your customer and treat them as people with intelligence. Always focus on one customer at a time. Make every customer feel special.
- You should give customer, their space and let them browse in peace. Always be available when he/she needs help.
- You should keep your store neat, clean and well organized. Make sure that every item has a price tag attached to it. Customers like to shop in a well organized store.
- You should make every customer's visit into your store a pleasant and memorable one, so that customer wants to come back and shop with you.

If you think you can

'YOU CERTAINLY CAN'

- You should always compliment on the purchase your customer has made. Always make it personalized by thanking the customer from your side and not the store's. Customer feels comfortable that way.
- You should always follow up every major purchase with a telephone call. Call the customer in a day or two to enquire about the purchase he/she has made. Always compliment again on their wise decision and take the opportunity to invite them back to shop.

Once you establish a comfort level with the customer, he/she will always come back and shop with you only. Even if you are busy with another customer he/she does mind waiting for you. Because they feel a personal connection with you and trust your judgement. When that happens with different customers, you can very comfortably call yourself 'Professional Sales Person'.

'Keep your eyes focused on the big objective'. 'To all the sales people'.

After working for twenty five years in retail environments in U.S.A., I enjoyed every minute of it. Every day was a new challenge for me and every day I learned something new from my customers, my superior and fellow associates.

Selling has given me a sense of accomplishment and personal satisfaction. You cannot learn selling in a school or a college but with personal experiences with the customers on the sales floor.

I am sure that when you establish yourself as a 'professional sales person', you will love every minute of it like I did.

This is my earnest wish and hope that this manual will help you to become a successful sales person.

'Remember: To be successful, you do not need a millionaire but you need to treat every customer as if he/she is worth a million'.

::--------::